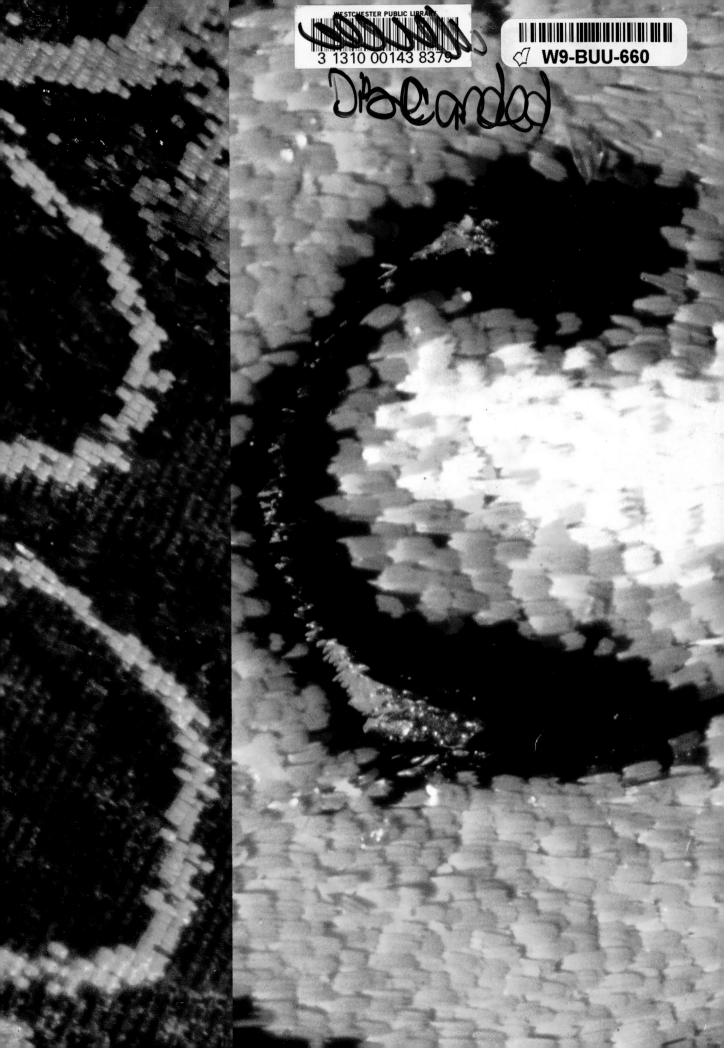

Hurt no living thing:

Ladybird, nor butterfly

Nor moth with dusty wing.

—Christina Rossetti

The *Butterfly* Alphabet

KJELL B. SANDVED

SCHOLASTIC
HARDCOVER

SCHOLASTIC INC.
New York

Library of Congress Cataloging-in-Publication Data

Sandved, Kjell Bloch
The butterfly alphabet : photographs / Kjell B. Sandved.
p. cm.
Includes index.
ISBN 0-590-48003-0
1. Butterflies—Pictorial works—Juvenile literature.
2. English language—Alphabet—Pictorial works—Juvenile literature.
[1. Butterflies. 2. Alphabet. M. Title.
QL543.S18 1996
595.78'9'0222—dc20   94-41514
CIP
AC

12 11 10 9 8 7 6 5 4 3 2 1   6 7 8 9/9 0 1/0

Printed in Singapore   46

First printing, March 1996

DEDICATED TO

MY LIFE-LONG FRIEND

Barbara Bedette

FOR HER INSPIRATION AND

LOVE OF NATURE'S

SMALL WONDERS

A NOTE TO READERS

Since ancient times, calligraphers have depicted the alphabet in many different ways. But no one had ever found all the letters as written by nature's own hand. One day many years ago, as I was looking through a microscope at a tropical moth, to my surprise I noticed a tiny, perfect letter **F** hidden on the wing. I was astounded and wondered if I could find other letters. Perhaps I could even find the entire alphabet in the wings of butterflies and moths! I decided that I was going to be the first to try.

Seeking and photographing the letters became my hobby and joy. Little did I imagine that it would take more than twenty-five years and visits to more than thirty countries to discover all the letters of the alphabet. I traveled to countries all over the world, from rain forests in South America, Africa, and New Guinea to the jungles of the Far East. Crawling on the ground, wading chest-deep in ponds, looking into blossoms, turning over leaves, and examining bark on trees, I sought out butterflies and moths everywhere. When I was finished, I had found some letters many times over.

In this book, you will find the picture of a butterfly or moth on one page, and the letter on the facing page. When you look closely, you may find the tiny letter hidden in the colorful pattern on the wing, but not always. In a few cases, the letter appears on the other side of the wing, so that you will not see it. But if you use your imagination, I am sure you will find other fascinating images in the patterns of the wing you can see.

Butterflies truly are the "symbol of the soul." Their delicate beauty and dancing flight from flower to flower help create love for nature and the desire to protect them. If their habitats are destroyed, they risk extinction. We must be careful to protect their meadows and forests.

And now, turn the pages of this book with a curious mind and a loving heart. Take delight in these small wonders. And come walk with me in this garden of butterflies. Nature's message is clear for all to see . . . *it is written on the wings of butterflies!*

Kjell B. Sandved
December 1995

On wings aloft across the skies —

An alphabet of butterflies.

BIRDWING BUTTERFLY

Each butterfly in secret brings

A letter hidden in its wings.

AFRICAN ATLAS MOTH

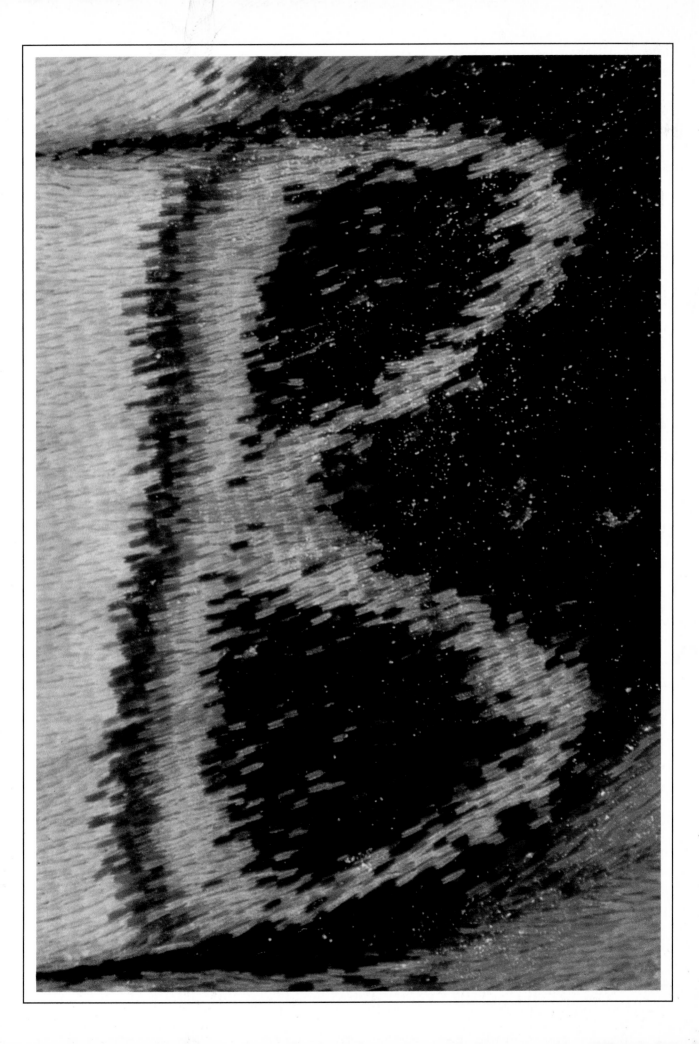

C

The rainbow gave to butterflies

Spots of color just their size.

CHRISTMAS SWALLOWTAIL BUTTERFLY

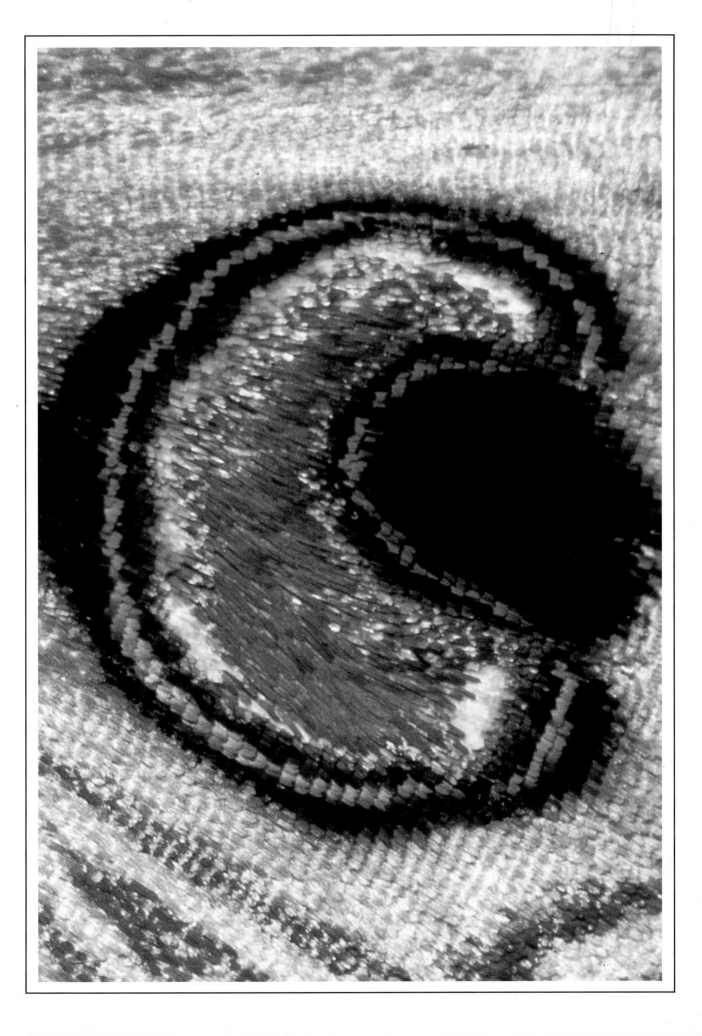

D

They dance among the forest lights

Like floating flower petal sprites.

SMALL APOLLO BUTTERFLY

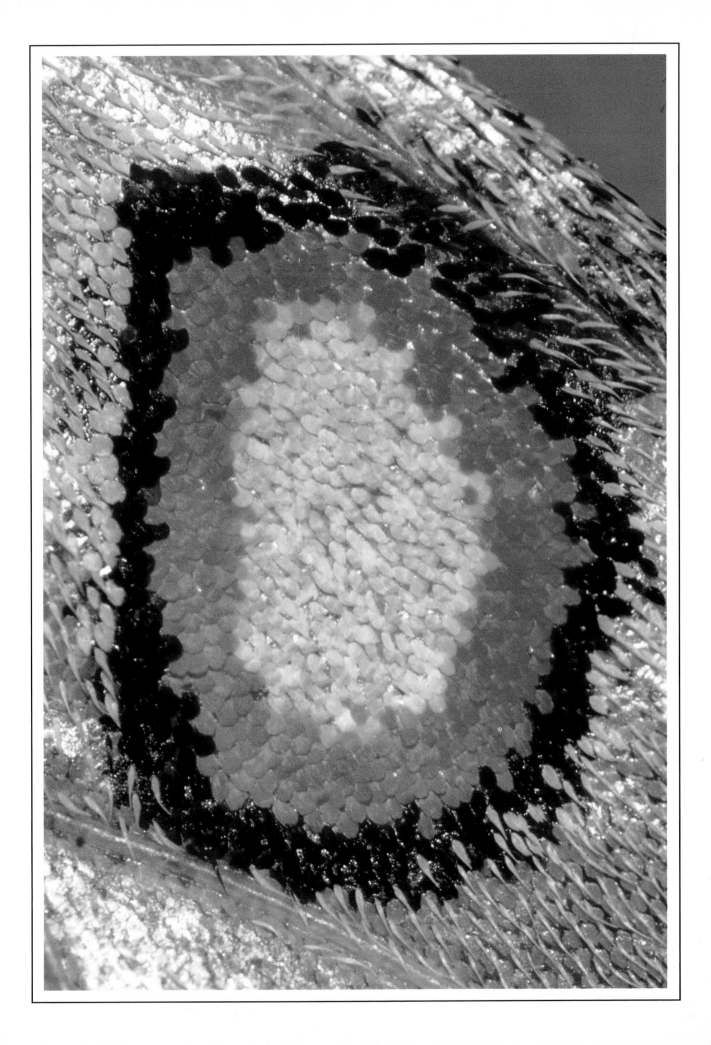

Each lifted by a gentle breeze,

They soar above with simple ease.

BLACK WITCH MOTH

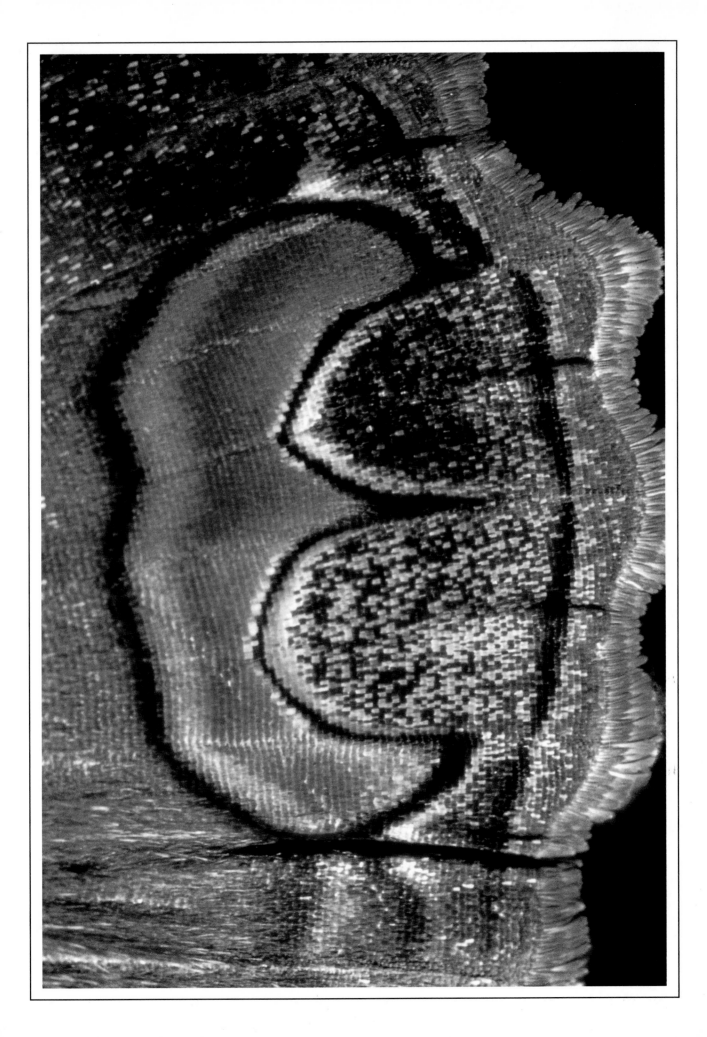

In their soundless flutter, see

A playful color melody.

SPHINX MOTH

Gilded like a jeweled crown

Or like a fancy wedding gown.

CATAGRAMMA BUTTERFLY

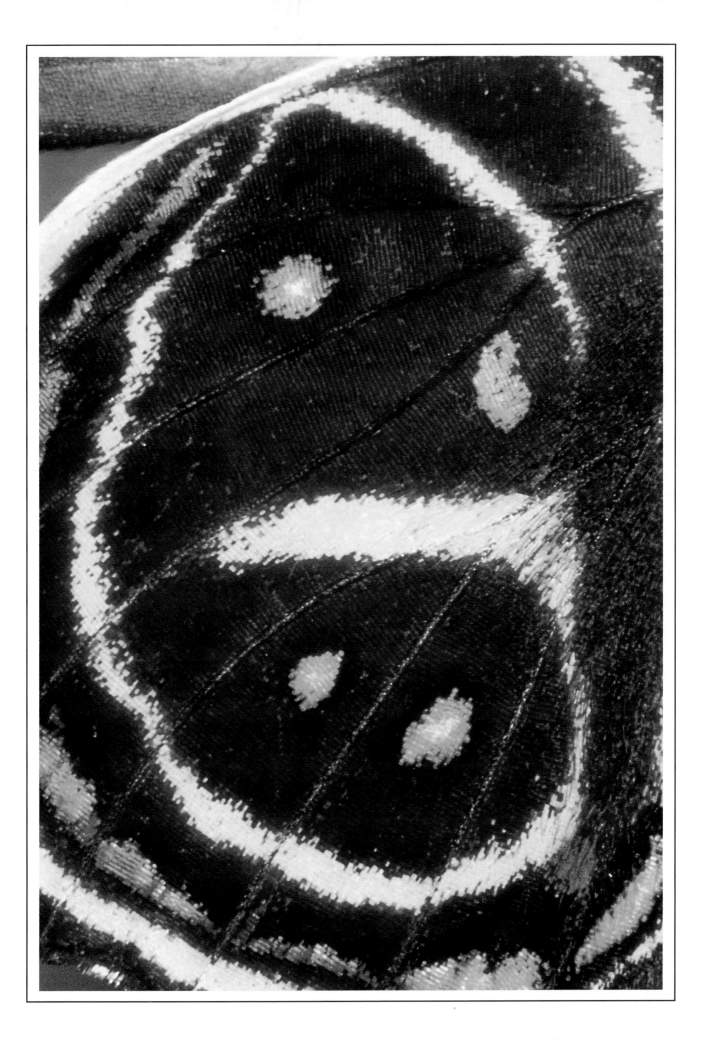

H

Each a tiny, stringless kite

Soaring up to treetop height.

METALMARK BUTTERFLY

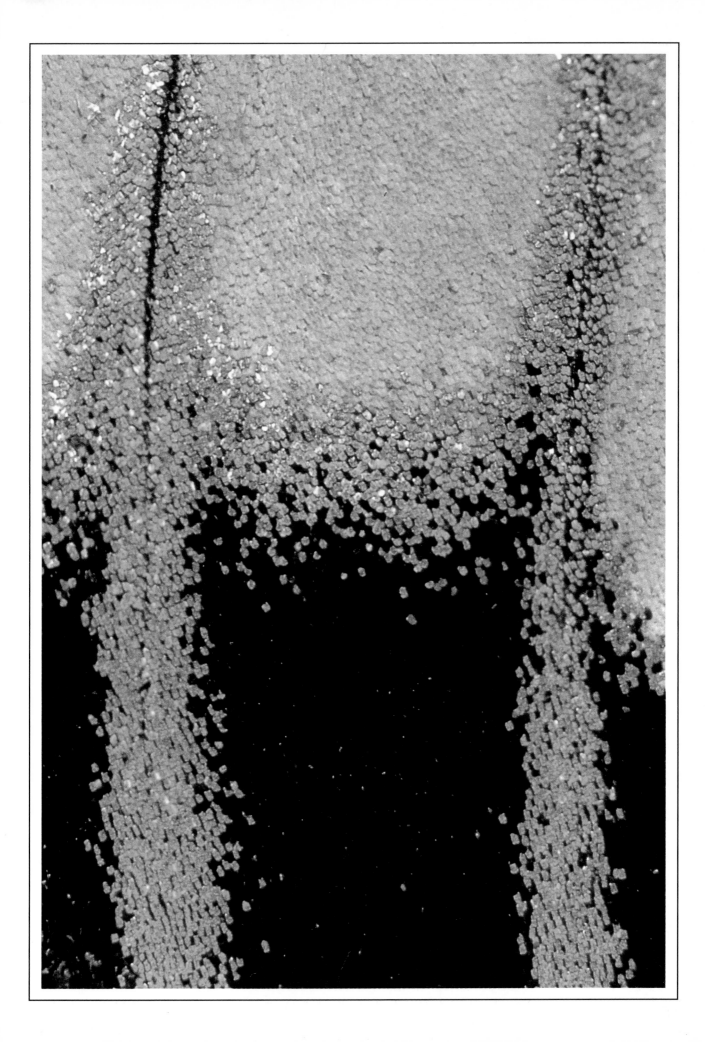

So innocent and unaware

Of the riches that they wear . . .

FEATHERWING METALMARK BUTTERFLY

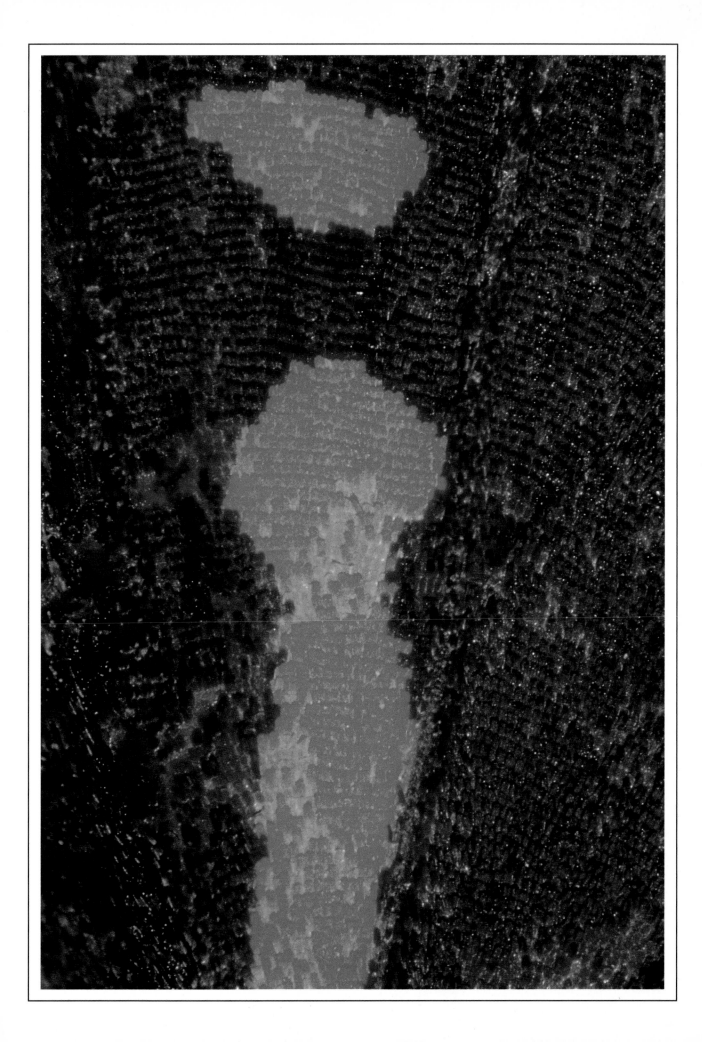

The joy a butterfly imparts

Awakens wonder in our hearts.

BLUME'S SWALLOWTAIL BUTTERFLY

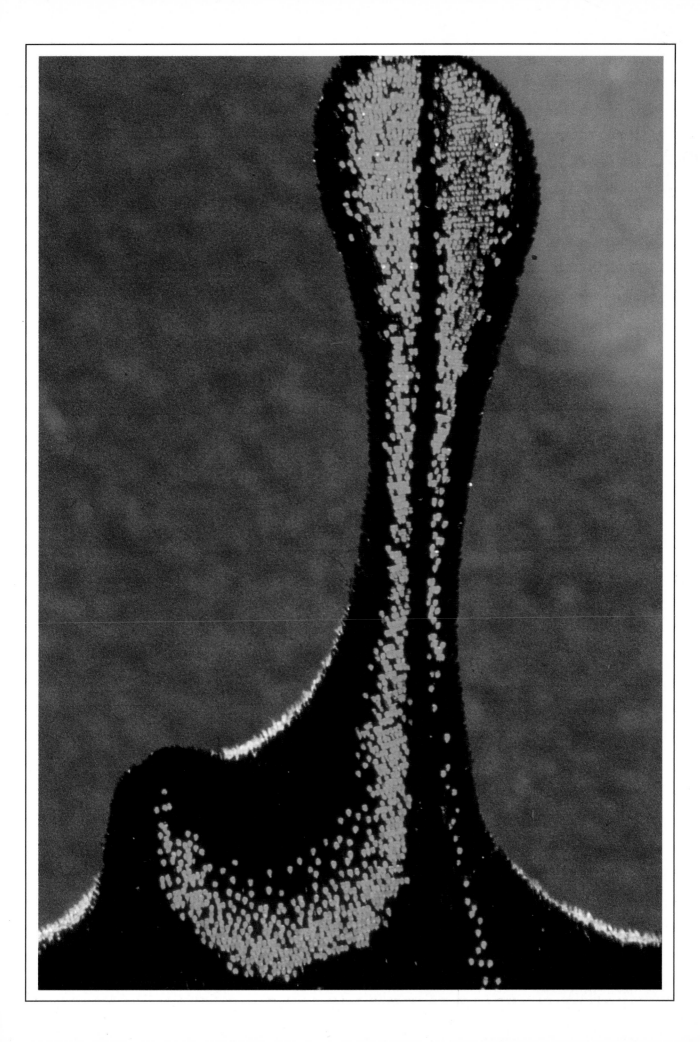

Behold their lovely, sparkling flight,

A kaleidoscope of colors bright.

CHARAXES BUTTERFLY

The flutter of their little wings

Inspires love for all small things.

METALMARK BUTTERFLY

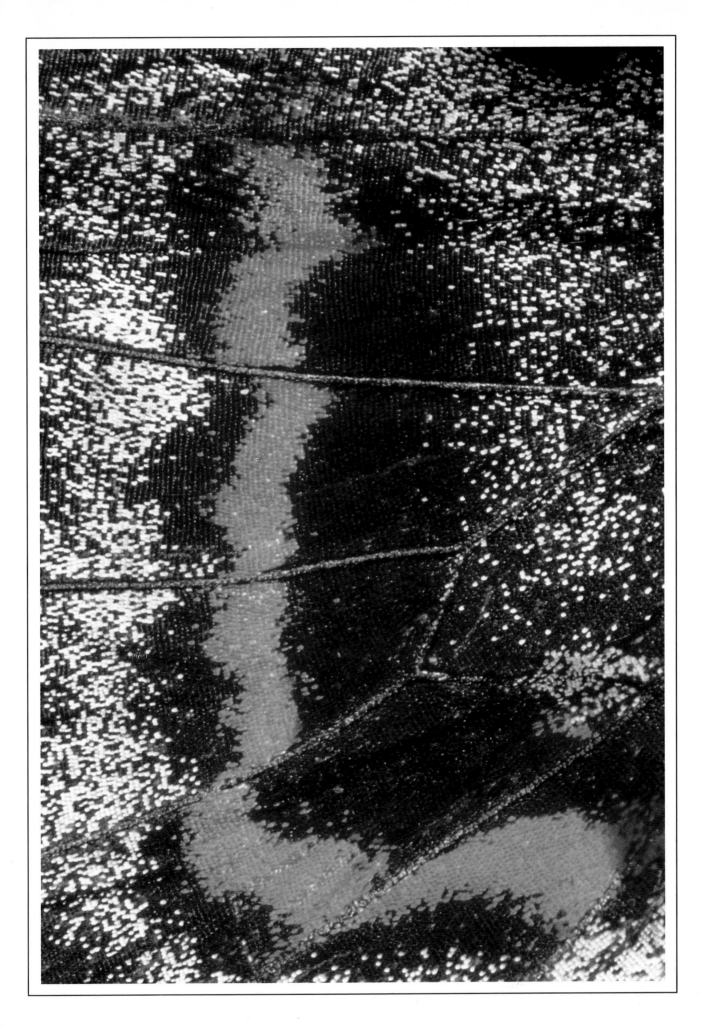

M

Merry nymphs in brilliant dress —

Messengers of happiness.

GREEN GEOMETRINE MOTH

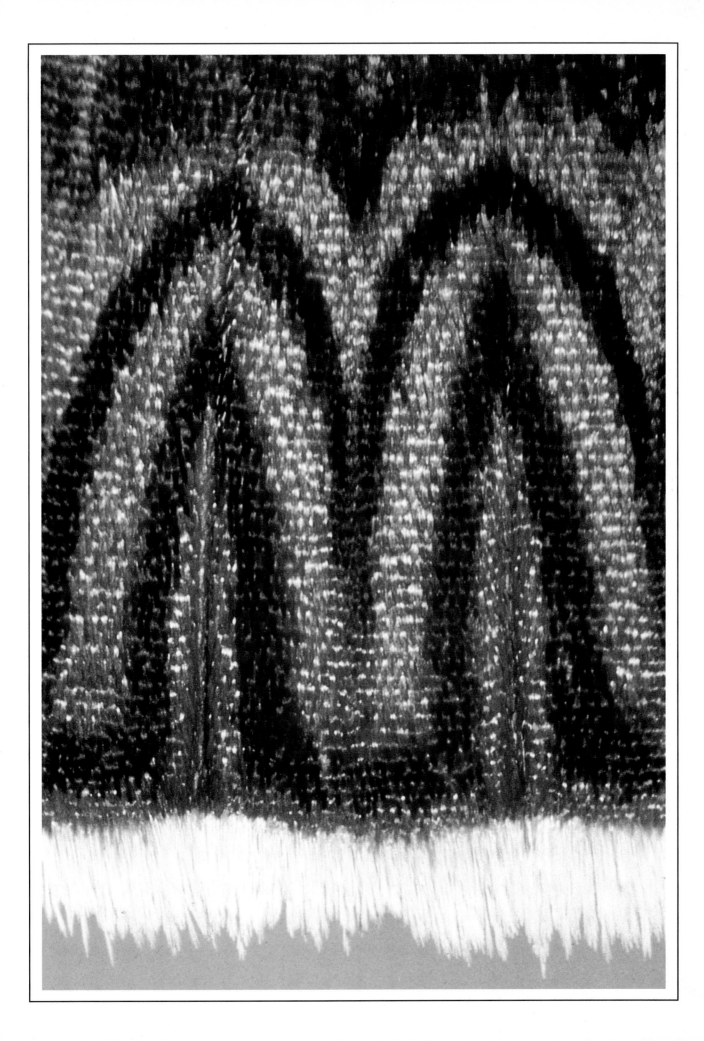

N

Butterflies enchant the hours,

Sipping nectar from the flowers.

TIGER ITHOMIINE BUTTERFLY

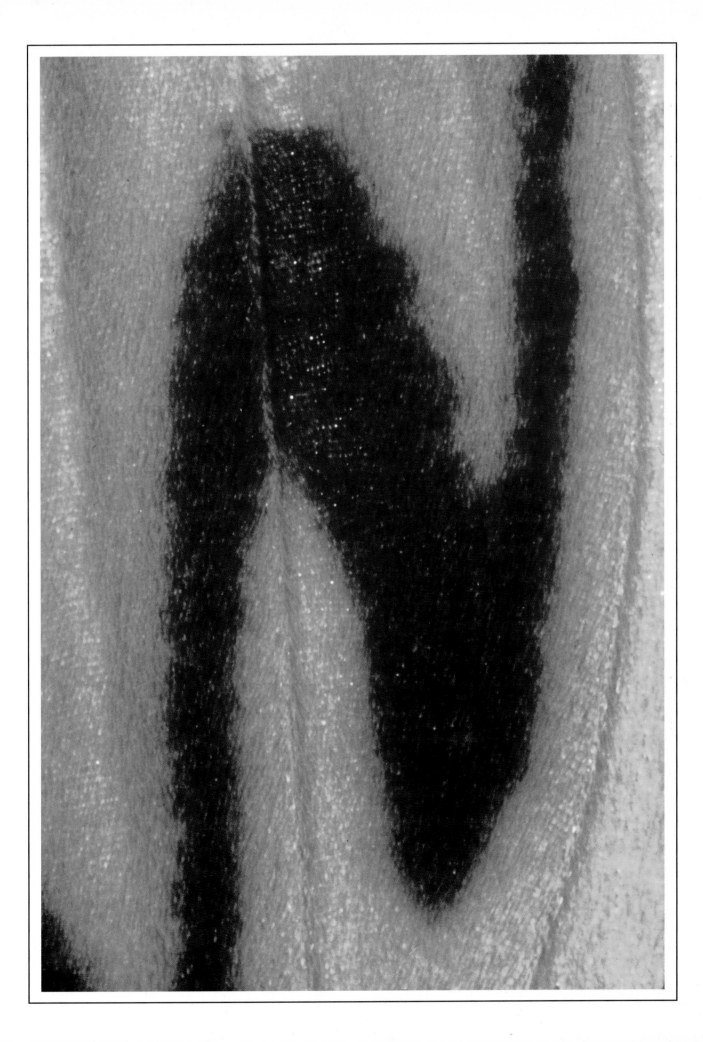

Ornaments floating in the air,

Charming all who see them there.

COMMON BUCKEYE BUTTERFLY

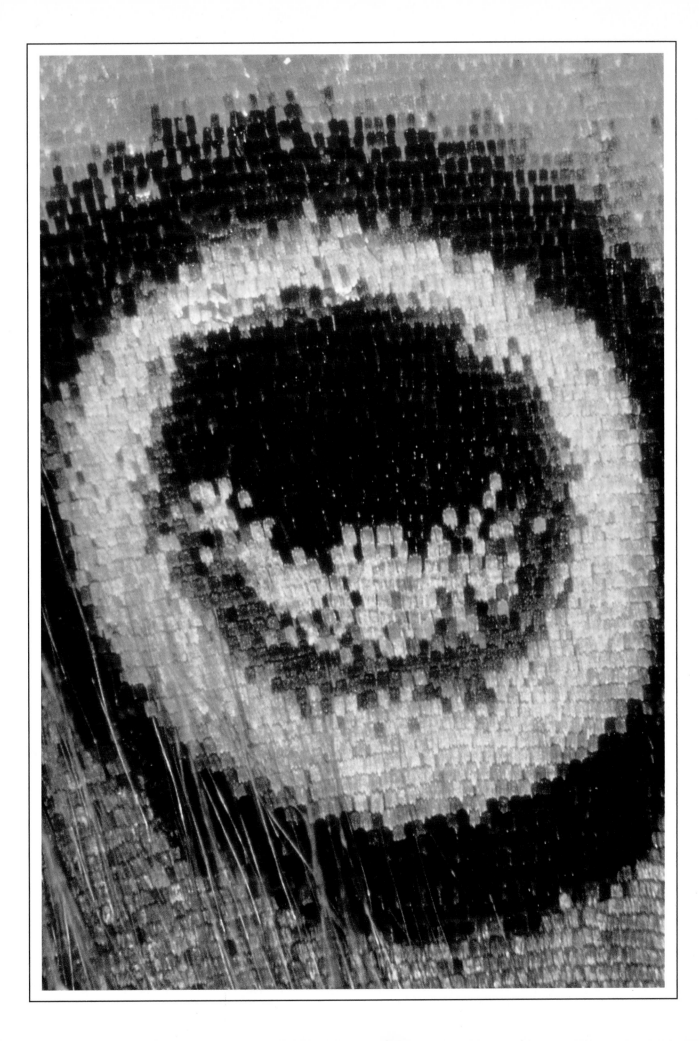

They tumble on the breeze all day

Like carnival acrobats at play.

GEOMETRID MOTH

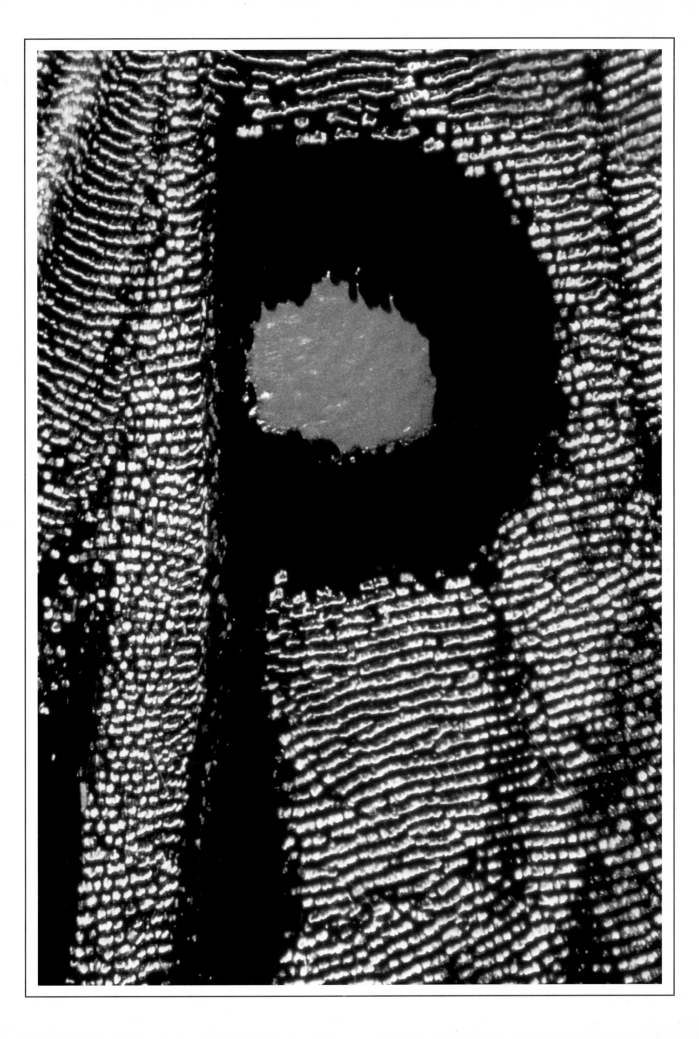

Quickly flitting, never still,

Free to wander where they will.

CLODIUS PARNASSIAN BUTTERFLY

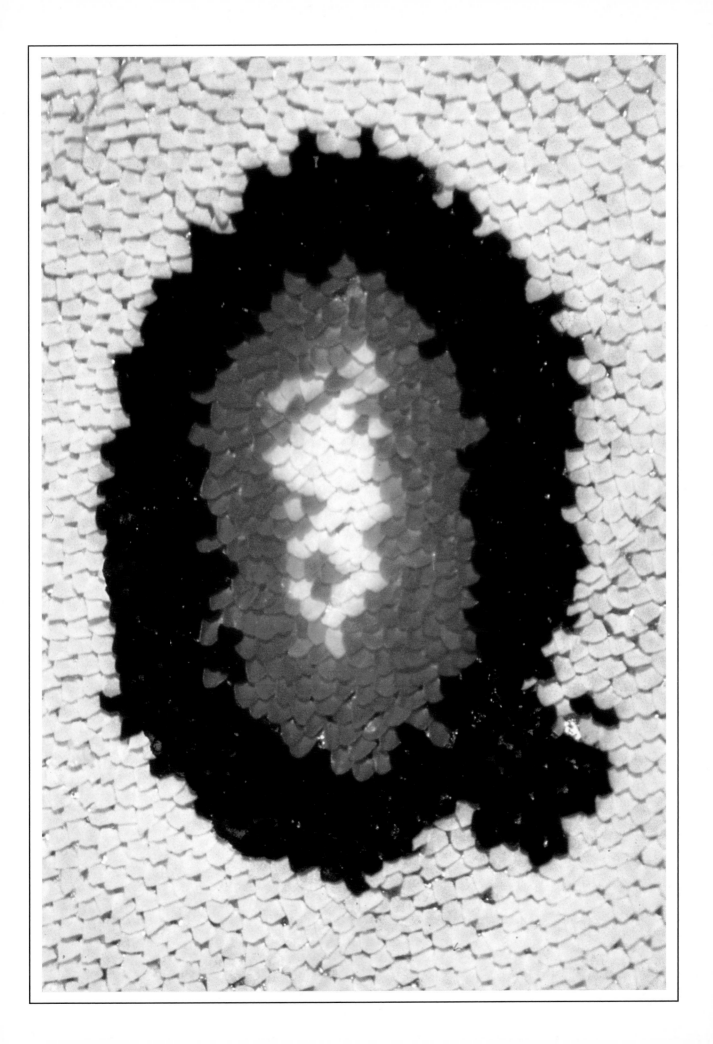

Radiant **colors catch the light —**

Imagination taking flight.

PLACENTIA TIGER MOTH

When butterflies in gardens meet,

Every flower smells more sweet.

SWALLOWTAIL BUTTERFLY

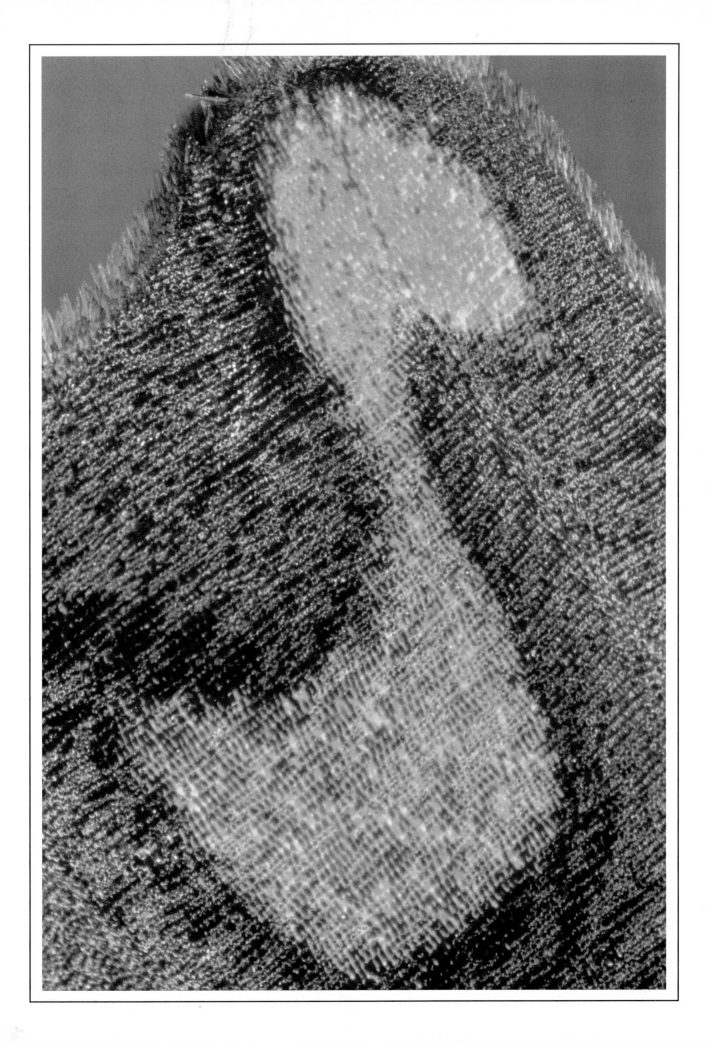

T

Nature's angels fill the skies

In twinkling butterfly disguise.

SMALL BROWN SHOEMAKER BUTTERFLY

Each morning, butterfly wings unfold

Their treasure: scarlet, blue, and gold.

AGRIAS BUTTERFLY

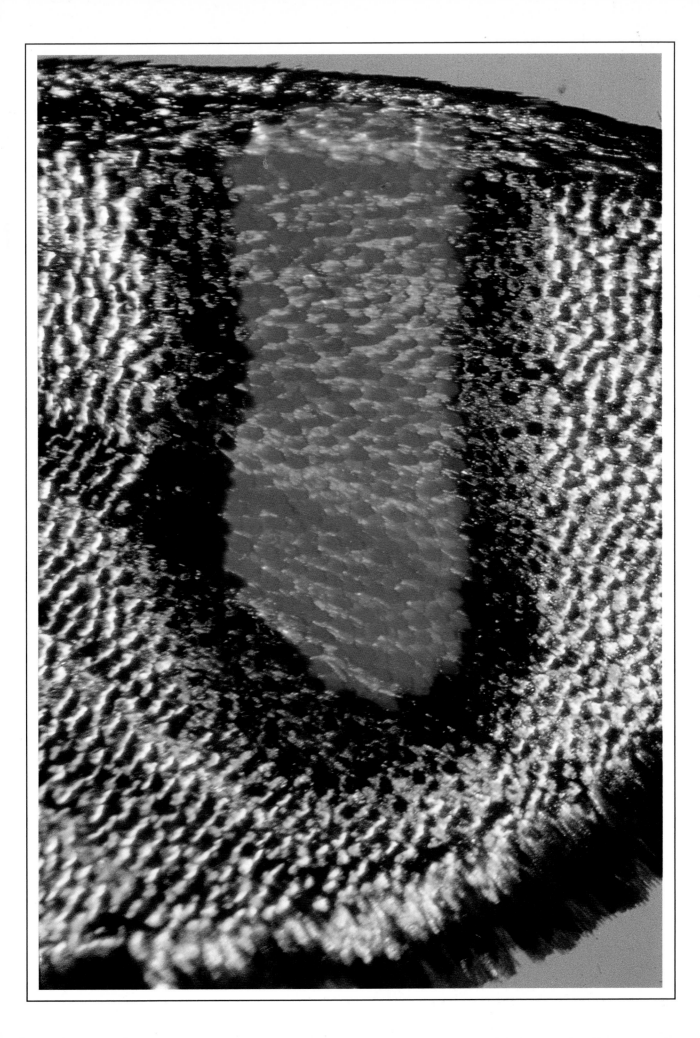

V

So simple is the majesty

Of nature's vibrant tapestry!

MORPHO BUTTERFLY

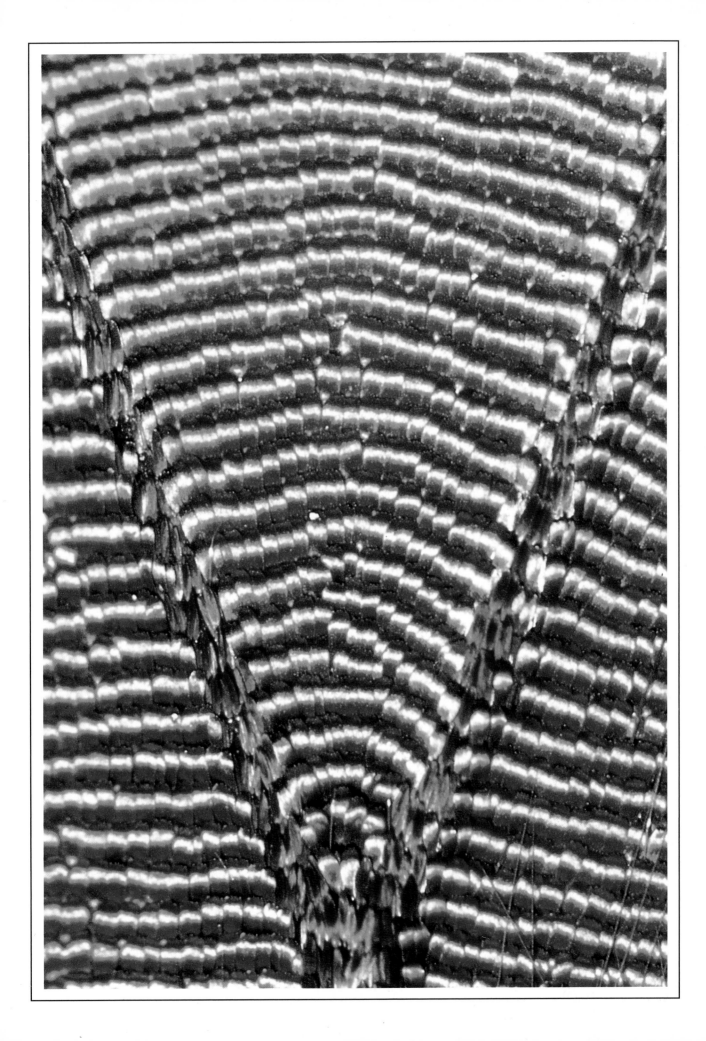

W

Delicate wings grace the air

As gently as a whispered prayer.

GEOMETRID MOTH

No delight is more exquisite

Than a surprise butterfly visit.

URANIID MOTH

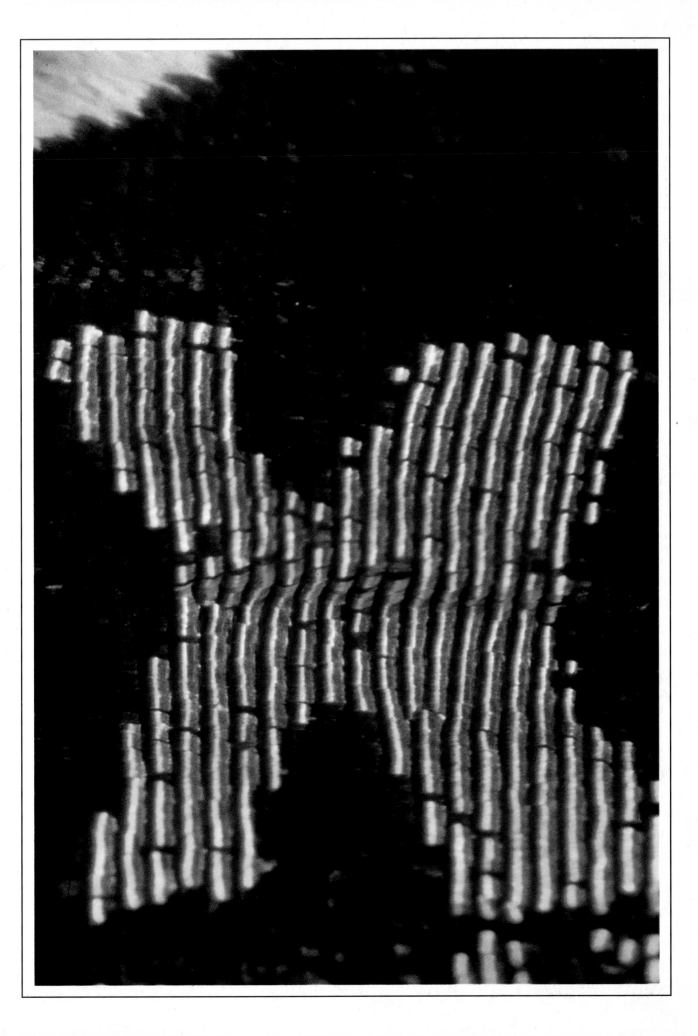

Y

Daydreaming, our fancy flies

Yonder with the butterflies.

FIERY CAMPYLOTES MOTH

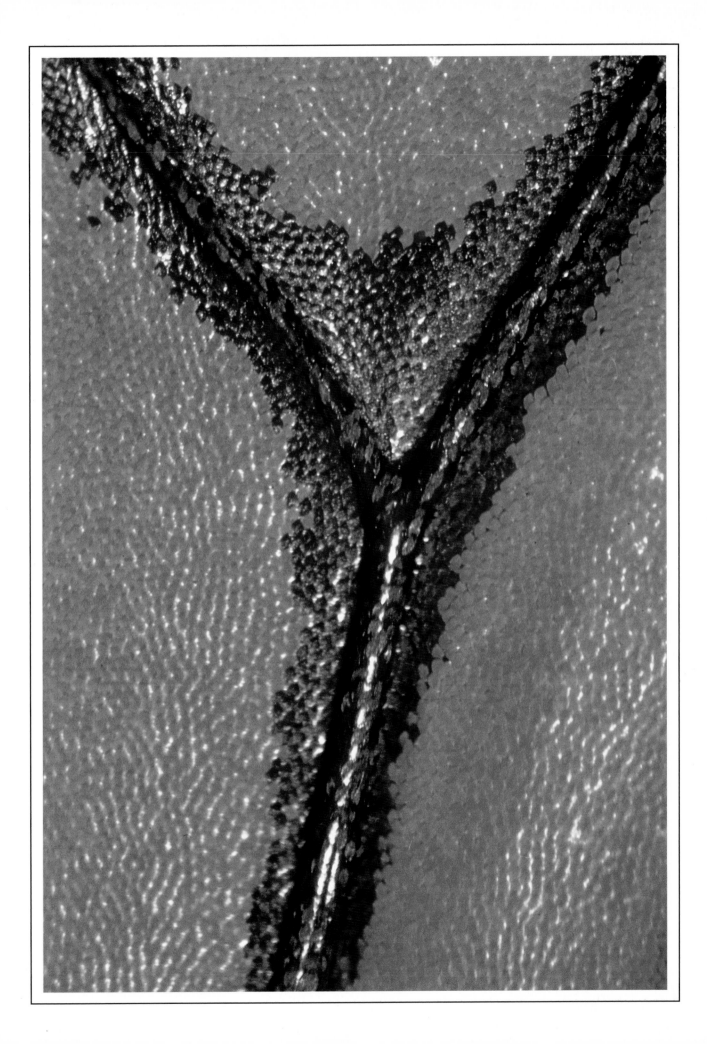

A butterfly wish — that all may see

And love their zigzag liberty!

BRAZILIAN 80 BUTTERFLY

ABOUT BUTTERFLIES

Do you know what a butterfly is? It is a caterpillar in a wedding gown!

Its life cycle includes four stages: egg, caterpillar, chrysalis, and adult butterfly. First the butterfly lays one or more tiny eggs on a leaf. Soon a small, hungry caterpillar crawls out of the eggshell and starts to eat the leaf. After the caterpillar has spent a few weeks eating and is fully grown, it settles down to spin a chrysalis, or cocoon, around itself. Inside this chrysalis, the caterpillar, which ate but did not drink, transforms itself — metamorphoses — in a miraculous way into a butterfly, which will drink but not eat.

Eventually, on a warm summer day, the chrysalis bursts open, and out comes a beautiful butterfly — the caterpillar in its wedding gown. Both male and female are arrayed in this beautiful way. Then, in a few short weeks, it fulfills the purpose of its life: to flutter from blossom to blossom, sipping nectar and pollinating flowers, and to find a mate and lay eggs before dying. With those eggs, the cycle will begin again.

What is the difference between butterflies and moths? In some ways, they are as different as night and day. Butterflies are active during the day, while moths are active at night. Butterflies are guided by sight, while moths are guided by scent. Butterflies have slender bodies, while moths' bodies are stout. But moths can be just as beautifully colored and fascinating to study as butterflies.

As you have seen in the close-up photographs in this book, butterfly and moth wings are made up of thousands of tiny scales overlapping one another like shingles on a roof. Butterflies and moths are part of the large insect order called *Lepidoptera*, which means "scaly winged." The scales are more than just beautiful. The colors and patterns are very important for butterfly survival. Butterflies use them to recognize one another when searching for mates. The markings also help defend them from their many predators, such as birds, bats, frogs, and even monkeys, that see a butterfly as a tasty meal. Bright, round "eyespots" (the letter **O**) may frighten away predators, or might cause them to attack a butterfly's wing instead of its vulnerable body. A butterfly might also startle a foe by suddenly flashing its bright wings and darting away. The subtle underwing markings serve as camouflage, helping butterflies blend in with their surroundings.

The variety of wing patterns is amazing. Even within one species, there are differences from male to female, from place to place, and from individual to individual. There are more than fifteen thousand different species of butterflies and over one hundred fifty thousand species of moths in the world, and every single individual is as different and unique as the fingerprints on your fingers.

The butterflies and moths in this book appear similar in size. But in nature, they range from just one inch to twelve inches across — even larger than this page!

ABOUT THE BUTTERFLIES IN THIS BOOK

I have done my best to correctly identify the common names and scientific family names of the butterflies and moths in this book. Often, a butterfly must be examined closely or even killed to make a precise identification. I did not capture the butterflies in a net or kill them, but photographed them during the cooler morning or late afternoon hours when they are naturally less active. Still, many flew away before I had time to identify them. In those cases, I have given the name of the butterfly's close relative, a sister or cousin, as it were. I am grateful to my friend Dr. Michael G. Emsley, Professor of Biology at George Mason University, Fairfax, Virginia, and to Dr. Paul A. Opler at the National Biological Service, Fort Collins, Colorado, for their valuable help.

A Birdwing Butterfly, PAPILIONIDAE (New Guinea). With a wingspan of five inches, the Birdwing has velvety black front wings with glossy lines, and hind wings with rows of pearly golden **A**'s.

B African Atlas Moth, SATURNIIDAE (Ghana). This beautiful moth, with resplendent gold, purple and brown designs, detailed eyespots, and sparkling, transparent patches, has one of the largest wingspans, of up to twelve inches.

C Christmas Swallowtail Butterfly, PAPILIONIDAE (West Africa). This Swallowtail, with gently scalloped hind wings, does not have the long tails which are typical of most Swallowtail butterflies.

D Small Apollo Butterfly, PAPILIONIDAE (Switzerland). The red circular designs of Apollo butterflies differ greatly from individual to individual. Varieties can be found in many climates, from tropical forests to Arctic mountain slopes.

E Black Witch Moth, NOCTUIDAE (Venezuela). These beautiful moths have ears on the sides of their bodies which sense the squeaks of predatory bats. During the day, they hide among dead foliage or bark.

F Sphinx Moth, SPHINGIDAE (Venezuela). Sphinx moths fly fast, reaching speeds of up to thirty miles per hour. Like hummingbirds, they hover in front of flowers with rapidly beating wings as they feed. They make a squeaking sound when handled.

G Catagramma Butterfly, NYMPHALIDAE (Brazil). This butterfly has a wingspan of only one inch. It feeds on rotting fruit, dung, and decaying matter rather than flower nectar.

H Metalmark Butterfly, RIODINIDAE (South America). This rain forest dweller feeds early in the morning, then rests on the underside of leaves. The blue markings are made of sparkling, mirror-like scales, which is how it got its name.

I Featherwing Metalmark Butterfly, RIODINIDAE (Guyana). The jet-black scales of this Metalmark are long like feathers.

J Blume's Swallowtail Butterfly, PAPILIONIDAE (Celebes, Indonesia). This Swallowtail has distinctive long tails. The upside-down **J** in one wing is mirrored in the upside-down **L** in the other.

K Charaxes Butterfly, NYMPHALIDAE (Africa). The three tails of the Charaxes butterfly form a beautiful **E**. Sometimes lovely hearts and faces appear in its wings.

L Metalmark Butterfly, RIODINIDAE (Peru). The shimmering colors of this Metalmark appear different from different angles. It sips juices from rotting fruit on stream banks.

M Green Geometrine Moth, GEOMETRIDAE (Colombia). This moth is a master of deception. White antennae and white lines in the wing distract birds from its vulnerable head. The brown areas make the moth look like dead leaves.

N Tiger Ithomiine Butterfly, NYMPHALIDAE (Equador). The bright red color and bold lines warn hungry birds that this butterfly tastes bad.

O Common Buckeye Butterfly, NYMPHALIDAE (Southern United States). These are also known as Peacock Butterflies. The magnificent eyespots scare away predators.

P Geometrid Moth, GEOMETRIDAE (Sri Lanka). The caterpillar, or larval, form of Geometrid moths, the Inchworm or Looper, makes loops with its body as it walks.

Q Clodius Parnassian Butterfly, PAPILIONIDAE (Canada). The wings of this butter-fly have long, hairlike scales which help it keep warm in the cool climate of its habitat.

R Placentia Tiger Moth, ARCTIIDAE (Eastern United States). The bright, striped pattern of this moth's wings have earned it the name Tiger Moth. In its larval stage, it is the Woolly Bear Caterpillar.

S Swallowtail Butterfly, PAPILIONIDAE (Kashmir). You can find the letters **I**, **O**, **L**, as well as **S** in this Swallowtail's hind wings.

T Small Brown Shoemaker Butterfly, NYMPHALIDAE (Guatemala). These butter-flies hide on decaying yellow leaves on the wet forest floor. During the cold season, they hibernate in clusters, or migrate to warmer places.

U Agrias Butterfly, NYMPHALIDAE (Argentina). The male Agrias has a patch of gold scales on its abdomen, which gives off perfume to attract females.

V Morpho Butterfly, MORPHIDAE (South America). The Morpho is distinctive for its brilliant blue color and quick, irregular flight in the bright sunlight of gaps in the rain forest canopy.

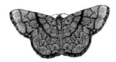

W Geometrid Moth, GEOMETRIDAE (Thailand). This moth is protected by blend-ing in with the dead leaves, bark, and mushrooms of its habitat.

X Uraniid Moth, URANIIDAE (Mexico). The feathery scales of this rapidly flying moth allow it to fly silently. It is active during the day, which is unusual for moths.

Y Fiery Campylotes Moth, ZYGAENIDAE (Nepal). This day-flying, sun-loving moth is only found at high altitudes in India, Nepal, and Tibet. The bright red colors warn birds that it tastes nasty.

Z Brazilian 80 Butterfly, NYMPHALIDAE (Brazil). Its name refers to the striking black and white markings on the underside of the wings, which may look like the numbers 80, 86, 88, or 89. It measures only one-and-a-half inches across.

The Butterfly Alphabet was inspired by Kjell B. Sandved's *Butterfly Alphabet* poster, pictured here, which received a Parents' Choice Award. For information about ordering the poster, call 1-800-ABC-WING.

The photographs in this book were created by Kjell B. Sandved using optical equipment he devised himself. To achieve sharp images of the tiny wing scales, Sandved attached special Zeiss microscope lenses to bellows. He set electronic strobe lights at specific angles to capture the colors. He used Kodachrome 25 ASA transparency color film, as well as color correcting filters.

The text type was set in Folio Light, Medium, and Bold. The display type was set in Cerigo Swash and Zapf International. Color separations were made by Bright Arts, Ltd., Singapore. Printed and bound by Tien Wah Press, Singapore. Production supervision by Angela Biola. Design by Marijka Kostiw. Printed on recycled paper.